The Trial of Lady Chatterley's Lover

D1328922

Also by SYBILLE BEDFORD

The Trial of Lady Chatterley's Lover

REGINA v. *PENGUIN BOOKS LTD* [1960]

SYBILLE BEDFORD

With an Introduction by
THOMAS GRANT

DAUNT BOOKS

This edition first published in
Great Britain in 2016 by
Daunt Books
83 Marylebone High Street
London W1U 4QW

1

This text originally appeared in *Esquire*, 1959–60.

A CIP catalogue record for this title is
available from the British Library.

ISBN 978 1 907970 97 9

Typeset by Antony Gray
Printed and bound by TJ International

www.dauntbookspublishing.co.uk

INTRODUCTION

IT IS RARE for a writer to invent a genre. Trial-writing existed in England before Sybille Bedford first set foot in the Old Bailey, but it was writing that was directed towards the preceding crime, or alleged crime, and the unravelling of the truth via the court process. The focus was on the victim, the act and the accused, and the journey towards conviction or acquittal. Sybille Bedford's great insight was that the trial itself should be the subject. Her gaze was fixed on the space bounded by the four walls of the court-room, the strange performance that makes up the trial, and the participants in a highly ordered ritual. The witnesses, the judge, the jury, the barristers and the defendant, alone in the dock, are all active and principal players in her dramas, thrown together by haphazard forces for a short period of intense interaction. Bedford's achievement was to treat the trial not as the resolution of prior events, but as *the* event.

That Bedford should have developed such an interest in the English trial process is in itself remarkable. Born into the German aristocracy before the First World War, and of mixed Catholic and Jewish heritage, her early life was that of the cosmopolitan itinerant. The rise of Nazism took her to America, where she remained throughout the Second War before settling back in Europe in the late 1940s. She had already written her masterpiece, the novel *A Legacy*, when she was commissioned to attend the trial for murder of the Eastbourne general practitioner, John Bodkin Adams, at the Old Bailey in 1957. The resulting book, *The Best We Can Do*, was revolutionary in its approach and focus. It remains the best full-length account of a criminal trial written in English. There followed a series of shorter accounts (published initially in various magazines) of some of the key criminal cases of the 1960s: the prosecutions of Penguin Books for publishing an unexpurgated edition of *Lady Chatterley's Lover*; of Stephen Ward for supposedly living off the immoral earnings of Christine Keeler and Mandy Rice Davies, of Jack Ruby (the assassin of Lee Harvey Oswald), and of the Auschwitz commandants.

The trial of *Regina* v. *Penguin Books Ltd* needs little introduction. It is perhaps the most (in)famous criminal prosecution in England in the twentieth century. The notion of a legal inquiry before an Old Bailey jury as to the obscenity or otherwise of a novel by D. H. Lawrence seems fantastical now but at the time it was treated by the defence as a case which was by no means a foregone conclusion. And so thirty-six 'expert' witnesses were called to speak to the literary, ethical and even spiritual qualities of the book. It was the evidence of these witnesses, a fascinating cross-section of contemporary intellectual life (Roy Jenkins, Rebecca West, E. M. Forster, Richard Hoggart . . .), which provided the meat of the trial, and also, in the hysterical and increasingly ineffectual attempts by the prosecution to cross-examine them, its humour.

Bedford's essay, published here for the first time since 1992, was one of many written in the immediate aftermath of the verdict. But, through a combination of cool observation, close attention to the actual words spoken in the interplay between counsel and the witnesses, and restrained outrage it remains the seminal account. For Bedford, commissioned by *Esquire* to attend the trial, this was not just another writing assignment. It was a public event which mattered; in a way the future direction of the intellectual and moral life of the country turned upon its outcome. In a later letter to her agent Bedford wrote: 'I felt so desperately strongly about it – it was like being in the war together – I sat with Ken Tynan and Penelope [Gilliatt] part of the time – shaking with anguish and fury . . . I hope it has not muddied the writing . . . '

In the event the account Bedford produced is a model of sinewed clarity. It is prose wrought from the discipline of the typewriter rather than the laxness of the word-processor. And re-reading it today, more than 50 years after the events it recounts, is a wholly successful exercise in time-travel to the foreign country of the past. The urgency remains undiminished.

Thomas Grant, 2016

The Trial of Lady
Chatterley's Lover

Lawyers have been known to wrest from reluctant juries triumphant verdicts of acquittal for their clients even when those clients were clearly and unmistakably innocent.

OSCAR WILDE

How beastly the bourgeois is especially the
     male of the species . . .
Let him meet a new emotion, let him be faced
     with another man's need.
Let him come home to a bit of moral
     difficulty.
Let life face him with a new demand on his
     understanding
And then watch him go soggy, like a wet
     meringue.
Watch him turn into a mess, either a fool
     or a bully.
Just watch the display of him, confronted with
     a new demand on his intelligence,
A new life-demand.

D. H. LAWRENCE

The Crown *v.* Penguin Books Limited
before Mr Justice Byrne and a jury
at the Central Criminal Court London
20 October–2 November 1960

LET THERE be no mistake: this was a criminal prosecution. It was entirely unlike the action on the same book between Grove Press Inc. and the Postmaster General that was heard before a judge in the United States District Court in 1959. Publication of an obscene article is a criminal offence in Britain, and before the new Act of Parliament was passed in July, 1959, there was no defence against it – other than a factual denial of having published; the author had no right to be heard in defence of his own book, nor had publishers, booksellers, critics or members of the general or specialised public. The penalty could be a prison sentence, and there was no maximum limit as to the number of years. The book did not have to be judged as a whole. The practice was to give juries passages marked by the prosecution or the police on which they had to decide whether the book was obscene or not, and that was that.

The new Act was designed to protect bona fide literature, and it took five years of devoted effort to get it passed. It tightened the powers against pornography, Judge Woolsey's dirt-for-dirt's-sake. It did not put through all that the reformers could have wished, but the best, in the circumstances, they could get. The most important new provisions of the Act are that the book must now be judged as a whole; that literary merit is a justification; and that the defence may call expert evidence.

Almost exactly one year afterward, two things happened. 1960 was the year of the seventy-fifth anniversary of D. H. Lawrence's birth and the thirtieth anniversary of his death; it was also the year of Penguin Books' twenty-fifth jubilee. They decided to round off their edition of Lawrence's works by publishing the unexpurgated version of *Lady Chatterley's Lover*. The authorities decided to prosecute. Penguin voluntarily delayed distribution and, not wishing to involve a bookseller, provided evidence of publication by handing over some copies to a police inspector by arrangement, and so offered themselves up as subjects of a test case.

The reaction of one section of the public was that this was plain incredible; had not the new Act been created to protect precisely this kind of book by this kind of author? They began to read or reread *Lady Chatterley's Lover* (the American edition was circulating in the country) and, reading, became aware that indeed a grave injustice was about to be committed. It seemed a monstrous irony that the authorities – who surely must have *some* duty to the public – should have acted against one of the very few writers of our time who bitterly protested against prostitution and perversion. Scores of eminent people wrote to Penguin, offering their testimony, and so began the mounting of the first full-scale literary trial in our legal history.

THE AUTHORITIES prepared by sending down to the Old Bailey Mr Justice Byrne – since retired – considered by the profession one of the best criminal judges in England (he tried Lord Haw-Haw), an Irishman and seemingly a man with little taste for fiction. The prosecution was entrusted to Mr Mervyn Griffith-Jones, Second Senior Counsel to the Crown at the Central Criminal Court, Eton, Cambridge, Coldstream Guards, and a veteran of many previous obscenity cases. What one could see of his face in court was framed by the wig: high cheekbones, a florid colour, a strong jaw and a thin mouth – the head of a conventionally handsome man. He neither stooped nor lounged.

The trial, like every major trial for a century, took place in Number 1 Court at the Old Bailey. (And as if to nudge, as it were, the historical undertones, Oscar Wilde's son, Mr Vyvyan Holland, was present the first day.) Number 1 is the largest courtroom in the building, which does not mean that it is not fairly cramped and small. It uncomfortably holds two hundred people, most of whom are unable to see *and* hear justice being done. The acoustics are wretched. The huge dock, solidly planted in the centre, successfully shuts off vision and sound.

The first move was the calling of the jury. Now, in the case of United States *v*. One Book Called *Ulysses*, the parties waived their right to a trial by jury, and Judge Woolsey commented on this as 'highly appropriate in a case involving books . . . a jury trial would have been extremely unsatisfactory, in fact an almost impossible way to deal with it . . . ' And, as it is ironical to remember in the light of what did happen, the defence in the present case is said to have shared that view; given the choice, counsel would have chosen trial by a judge. But in English law there is no actual choice; the magistrate must make the final decision; in the case of Penguin it was trial by jury.

An English jury is a permanent unknown quantity, a number of men and women chosen at random and finally by lot, about whom nothing is known, or allowed to be known, by anyone concerned. They are – forever – so many names and faces. (There is an unwritten law that a jury cannot be spoken to afterwards, and even if some-body did try to speak to them – as some of the press did in this case – the jury would not answer, and if it did answer nobody would dare to print it.) The fine art of weeding out a jury, as is done in the United States, is no longer practised in England. The defence has still the right to object to up to seven jurors without giving a reason, the peremptory challenge as it is called. But it is an obsolescent right, very rarely used nowadays.

Here it *was* used. Counsel made some slight sign and the Clerk said to the man who had just been marched into the jury box, 'Will you step down, please,' and the man did. He left the box. We all looked at him. Why? He had been the fourth or fifth man called; the box went on filling up; the twelfth and last juror was already halfway through his oath when there was another last-instant rejection. Amen said, and it would have been too late. That last man had been making a hash of trying to read his printed formula.

Now, the woman who was drawn in the last man's stead, and who was to become the twelfth acting juror in this trial, was a most educated-looking woman, with an alive and responsive face, and she may well have been the kingpin in the decision of that jury. Of course we shall never know . . .

Mr Griffith-Jones, opening for the Crown, addressed them. His evidence, he said, would be this book: *Lady Chatterley's Lover*. Penguin proposed to publish it at the price of 3/6, and indeed had printed 200,000 copies of it for sale. His voice was thin, clear and slow, and at this stage neutral, level. He explained the law as it stood now.

' "An article shall be deemed obscene if its effect, taken as a whole, is such as to tend to deprave and corrupt persons who are likely, having regard to all relevant circumstances, to read the matter contained in it." ' There was, however, another Section of the Act which said that it was not an offence to publish ' "If it is proved that the article is for the public good, on the ground that it is in the interest of science, literature, art or learning or other objects of general concern." '

The jury would have to give one verdict, but they would really have two questions to decide. One, whether the book was obscene; two, if so, whether its publication was justified as being for the public good. 'If you find the book is not obscene, that is an end of this matter and you must acquit. But if you find that it *is* obscene, then you have to go on to consider – is it proved that publication is in the interest of literature, art and so forth . . .

'A point you have to consider is how freely the book is going to be distributed. Is it a book published at £5 a copy as a historical volume, or is it a book widely distributed at a price the merest infant can afford?

'When you have read this book, you may think that it sets upon a pedestal promiscuous and adulterous intercourse, commends sensuality almost as a virtue, and encourages and advocates vulgarity of thought and language.'

Mr Griffith-Jones went on more emotionally: 'You may think one of the ways you can test this book is to ask yourself the question: would you approve of your own son and daughter – because girls can read as well as boys – reading this book? Is it a book you would have lying in your own house? Is it a book you would wish your wife or your servant to read?

'Members of the jury, you may think that the book is a picture of little else than vicious indulgence in sex and sensuality. I wish to concede that D. H. Lawrence is a world-recognised writer; I also concede, though not to such a great extent, that there may be some literary merit in this book, not to put it any higher.

'The book is about a young woman whose husband was wounded in the First World War so that he was paralysed from the waist downwards and unable to have sexual intercourse. I invite you to say that in effect the book is a description of how that woman, deprived of sex from her husband, satisfied her sexual desires – a sex-starved girl and how she satisfied that starvation with a particularly sensual man who happened to be her husband's gamekeeper.'

In a voice quivering with thin-lipped scorn,

Mr Griffith-Jones went on: 'There are thirteen passages of sexual intercourse in this book. The curtain is never drawn. One follows them not only into the bedroom, but into bed, and one remains with them there. The only variation between all thirteen occasions is the time and the place where it happens. So one starts in my lady's boudoir; one goes to a hut in the forest with a blanket laid down on the floor. We see them doing it again in the undergrowth, in the forest amongst the shrubbery, and again in the undergrowth in the pouring rain, both of them stark naked and dripping with raindrops. One sees them in the keeper's cottage: first in the evening on the hearthrug; then we have to wait until dawn to see them doing it again in bed. Finally we move the site to Bloomsbury, and we have it all over again in a Bloomsbury boarding house.

'That is the variation – the time and the place where it happens with the emphasis always on the *pleasure*, the *satisfaction*, the *sensuality* . . .

'Sex, members of the jury, is dragged in at every opportunity, even the girl's father, a Royal Academician, introduces a description of his legs and loins. The book says little about the character of any of these people; they are little more than bodies which continuously have sexual intercourse with one another. The plot, you may find, is little more than padding, until we reach the hut again, the cottage or the undergrowth in the forest . . . '

The jury sat through this blank-faced as juries are apt to sit. Then came the shock tactics: the passage in the prosecution speech which is by now well-known, the four-letter-word count.

'The word "fuck",' said Mr Griffith-Jones, 'appears thirty times. The word "cunt" fourteen times. The word "balls" thirteen times; "shit" six times; "arse" and "piss" three times apiece.'

This was flung across the court with deliberate brutality. And we were shocked. Not because of the words – the words, paradoxically enough, are common-place in an English court of law; we are much less mealy-mouthed in that than many of the Continental courts – but shocked by the staggering insensitiveness of this approach, the bookkeeper's approach, the line of attack. So this was to be the quality of the stand against a work by D. H. Lawrence.

An American writer, who was next to me, said, 'Why this is going to be the upper-middle-class English version of our Tennessee Monkey Trial.'

The prosecution speech ended by pointing out

that Penguin stated it had taken thirty years for it to be possible to publish the unmutilated version of *Lady Chatterley's Lover* in this country. 'You, members of the jury,' Mr Griffith-Jones said in a tone both ominous and smug, 'will have to say whether it *has* taken thirty years, or whether it will take still longer.'

Then the prosecution called their one and only witness, a policeman. Yes, he said, he had been given a dozen copies of the book in the Penguin offices. (This was formal evidence of publication.)

The chief witness, the book itself, was still unread; and before reading it the jury had to hear the opening speech by the defence. Penguin had briefed a dazzling team of counsel. The leader was Mr Gerald Gardiner QC,* one of the great silks of the London Bar, making one of the largest, perhaps the largest, income that it is possible to make there these days. Mr Gardiner is a Quaker, a law reformer and a man recognised for his high principles. His court style is unemotional, cool, undramatic; he's the man who appeals to reason. His juniors were Mr Jeremy Hutchinson and Mr Richard Du Cann, two distinguished barristers in

---

* The future Lord Chancellor.

their own right. Mr Hutchinson was himself brought up within an inner circle of the English world of letters, his father and mother having been patrons of the arts and friends of the writers of their time, George Moore, the Woolfs, Aldous Huxley, D. H. Lawrence . . .

This is how Gerald Gardiner began. He spoke gently, one might say compassionately. 'You have been told that this book is full of descriptions of sexual intercourse – and so it is. That it is full of four-letter words – and so there are.

'You may ask yourself at once: how comes it that reputable publishers, apparently after considerable thought and quite deliberately, are publishing an appalling book of the nature which has been described to us? . . . Penguin Books began in 1935 under a man called Lane, a man who thought that people like himself who were not very rich should be able to buy books. They started with a novel and some detective stories, then came classics and translations of masterpieces of literature, all costing sixpence. Twenty-five years later they had sold 250,000,000 books; they had published the whole of Shakespeare, most of Shaw; they had published fourteen books by D. H. Lawrence, and now they intended to publish the rest, including *Lady Chatterley's Lover*. This book has had unfortunately a history . . . ' It was written in 1928; it had not been possible to publish it at that time. 'There are many books circulating in London now which nobody would have thought ought to have been printed even twenty years ago.' There had been expurgated editions of *Lady Chatterley*, and there would have been nothing to stop Penguin years ago from publishing one, but they had always refused to publish a mutilated book. The expurgated edition was not the book Lawrence wrote. One could have expurgated editions of *Hamlet* and of the *Canterbury Tales*, but they would not be the books Shakespeare or Chaucer wrote.

The dock in this trial, said Mr Gardiner, was empty. The Crown had decided to prosecute Penguin merely as a company, and not the individual directors responsible. 'But there is nothing to stop them from what they frequently have done before. Possibly the prosecution thought that a jury might come to a verdict of Guilty rather more readily if the dock were empty than if they had someone sitting there.'

He then read dictionary definitions of To Deprave and To Corrupt. ' "To make morally bad; to pervert; to deteriorate; to make rotten; to infect, taint; to render unsound, to debase, to defile . . . " ' Strong words, and, as Mr Gardiner at once pointed out, 'So for a book to be obscene within the meaning of the law, it must obviously effect a change of character, a leading on of the reader to do something wrong which he would not otherwise have done.

'When you have read the book you will see certain things which the author was aiming at . . . Mr Griffith-Jones has suggested that this was a book which contained thirteen descriptions of physical intercourse, and the only variation between them was the time and place. I would suggest that you will find exactly the opposite. Here is a book about England of the Twenties . . . Lawrence's message is that the society of his day was sick, the result of the machine age and the importance which everybody attached to money, and to the extent to which mind had been stressed at the expense of the body, and that what we ought to do was to re-establish the personal relationships. And one of the greatest things, the author thought, was the relationship of a man and a woman in love, and their physical union formed an essential part of a relation which was normal and wholesome and not something to be ashamed of, but something to be discussed openly and frankly . . . Now if a man is going to write a book of that kind, and deal with the physical relation between the sexes, it is necessary to describe what he means.

'I submit that the descriptions of physical union were necessary for what Lawrence was trying to say.

'It is quite true that the book includes what are called four-letter words, and it is quite plain that what the author intended was to drag these words out of the rather shameful connotation which they had achieved since Victorian times. The attitude of shame with which large numbers of people have always viewed sex in any form has reduced us to the position where it is not at all easy for fathers and mothers to find words to describe to their children the physical union. The author thought that if he used what had been part of our spoken speech for about six hundred years, he could purify it . . . Whether he succeeded or not in his attempt to purify these words by dragging them into the light of day, there is nothing in the words themselves which can deprave or corrupt. If these words can deprave or corrupt, then ninety-five percent of the Army, Navy and Air Force are past redemption.

'Whole parts of the book may (and I do not doubt will) shock you; but there is nothing in the book which will in fact do anybody any harm. No one would suggest that the Director of Public Prosecutions would become depraved by reading the book, nor counsel, nor witnesses; no one would suggest that the judge and jury would become corrupted; it is always someone else, it is never ourselves!'

When Mr Gardiner had done, it was already afternoon, and the Judge said that the question now was how the reading was to be arranged. Mr Gardiner stepped forward, and so did Mr Griffith-Jones, and the following exchange took place.

Mr Gardiner: 'I understand the usual practice has been for the jury to take the book home.'

The Judge: 'I don't think I'm in agreement with that.'

The Judge looked an elderly gentleman, with a polite, dry voice; a wizened bit of face looked out from the full wig, Upright, he gave the impression old judges sometimes give, of a husk, light as kindling, under the scarlet robes.

Mr Gardiner: 'The jury rooms are jolly

uncomfortable. There are hard wooden chairs, and anything more unnatural than twelve men and women sitting on hard chairs around a table reading cheek by jowl in one another's presence is hard to imagine.'

The Judge tilted his head.

Mr Gardiner stood hunched up and tall. His face looked flexible, yet expressionless, and quite grey.

Mr Griffith-Jones: 'I have no wish to cause the jury any discomfort, but, in my submission, for them to read the book in the jury room is the proper way.'

Mr Gardiner: 'When you read, what you read is private to the author and you. Besides some people read more slowly than others—'

The Judge (quietly): 'In my experience, books are read in court.' Here the Clerk put his head above the dais. Confabulations. 'The Clerk does not agree that the jury rooms are uncomfortable.' Pause. 'I have never been in a jury room myself.'

Mr Gardiner: 'The average rate of reading is about two hundred words a minute . . . What would happen when one member of the jury has finished reading and others have not?'

The Judge (to the jury box): 'I am very sorry, I don't want to put you to any kind of discomfort, but if you were to take this book home you might have distractions.'

So the jury was directed to present themselves next morning, and the case was adjourned.

WHEN THE CASE resumed one week later on Day Two, as they call it, the place was filled with men and women who looked each more like themselves than it is customary for any multitude to do: the expert witnesses. Rumours as to who was going to appear had been circulating for some months. In the press, names were piled on speculative names. In fact, the actual list was unknown, and, what's more, remained so until the last witness had showed up on the last day. The solicitors responsible for organising the defence had kept it absolutely quiet. One popular paper spread the startling news that a fleet of London taxis was standing by to convey the poets of England from where they might lurk to the Old Bailey. As it turned out, the actual selections were much more subtle, much more effective and much more *terre à terre*.

The day began with Mr Griffith-Jones asking for the witnesses to be out of court during each other's testimony. Mr Gardiner objected that this was not the custom as far as experts were concerned. Mr Justice Byrne ruled that if there was no agreement on this point by the two sides, the custom was for the witnesses to stay out. A number of men and women thereupon withdrew.

How does one give evidence as to literary merit in a court of law? We were soon to hear. The first witness called was Mr Graham Hough, the literary critic and D. H. Lawrence specialist, Lecturer in English and Fellow of Christ's College, Cambridge.

Mr Gardiner: 'When did you first read the unexpurgated edition of *Lady Chatterley's Lover*?'

Mr Hough: 'In about 1940.' (This question was put to everyone, and all, whatever their upbringing or generation, had at one time or another read an underground copy.)

Mr Gardiner: 'Will you tell us something about Lawrence's place in English literature?'

Mr Hough: 'He is generally recognised as being one of the most important novelists of this century. I should put him with Hardy and with Conrad and George Eliot. I do not think that is seriously disputed.'

'How many books have been written about D.H.L.?'

'About eight hundred published.'

'How do you rank *Lady Chatterley*?'

'I don't think it's the best of Lawrence's novels, but not the least good either. About fifth place. He wrote nine.'

'Will you tell us what is the theme or meaning of this book?'

' . . . An attempt to give a sympathetic understanding to a very painful, intricate human situation. The book is in fact concerned with the relationships between men and women, with their sexual relations, and with the nature of marriage – all matters of great importance to us all.'

Mr Gardiner: 'It has been claimed that sex is dragged in at every opportunity and the plot is little more than padding.'

'I totally disagree. If true, this would be an attack on the integrity and honesty of the author. But it is quite false. In the first place, it is a matter of simple numerical proportion – the sexual passages occupy no more than about thirty pages of the whole book, a book of some three hundred pages. No man in his senses is going to write a book of three hundred pages as mere padding . . . And then the literary merit of the non-sexual passages is very high.'

Mr Gardiner: 'It has been suggested that

the book puts upon a pedestal promiscuous and adulterous intercourse.'

Mr Hough: 'Promiscuity hardly comes into it. It is very much condemned by Lawrence. It is true that at the centre of the book there is an adulterous situation – that is true of a great deal of the literature of Europe.'

'It has been said that the only variation in the scenes of intercourse is in the places they take place. Do you agree?'

'No, I don't! They show the development of Connie Chatterley's awareness of her nature. They are not repetitive. They are different and necessary to the author's purpose.'

Mr Gardiner: 'How far are the descriptions of intercourse relevant or necessary?'

'They are extremely necessary. Lawrence was trying to show sexual relationships more clearly than is usually done in fiction. Lawrence was making a bold experiment.'

'A what?' said the Judge.

'A bold experiment.'

'A bold experiment,' repeated the Judge as he wrote it down.

Mr Gardiner: 'How far are the four-letter words relevant or necessary?'

Mr Hough: 'May I answer that by explaining why they are in? In Lawrence's view, there is no proper language to talk about sexual matters. They are either discussed in clinical terms, which deprive them of all emotional content, or they are described in words that are usually thought to be coarse or obscene. He wished to find a language in which sex could be discussed plainly and not irreverently, and to do this he tried to redeem the normally obscene words by using them in a context that is entirely serious. I don't myself think that this is successful, but that is what he was trying to do. In trying to treat sex in this way, Lawrence had few precedents before him. He had to try to find a way through.'

Mr Gardiner: 'Do you spend a great deal of your time teaching young people?'

Mr Hough: 'I do.'

'And have you a daughter of eighteen and a son of twelve?'

'I have.'

So far, so good. Mr Hough had given his answers with thoughtful care. The jury had been sitting through their course in literary criticism with non-committal attention. Now came the first cross-examination.

Mr Griffith-Jones: 'Do you know a lady called Esther Forbes?'

Mr Hough: 'No. I'm afraid not.'

'Do you know a lady called Katherine Anne Porter?'

'A writer of short stories. American . . . Very distinguished.'

'Are you familiar with a magazine called *Encounter*?'

'*Encounter*? Yes, I am.'

'Is *Encounter* a serious publication?'

Mr Hough: 'Reasonably so.' (Laughter, instantly suppressed, in one section of the court; stony faces in the rest.)

Mr Griffith-Jones: 'Would you agree with this American lady writing in *Encounter* that this novel is "a dreary, sad performance, with some passages of unintentionally hilarious low comedy", and "written with much inflamed apostolic solemnity"?'

Mr Hough: 'I think that is an eccentric opinion.'

Mr G.-J. (quickly): 'Because you do not agree with it? Do you agree with this view of Lady Chatterley, ". . . she is merely a moral imbecile . . . she is stupid"?'

'Connie is not stupid; she is an emancipated

young woman of the period, friendly, warm-hearted, patient—'

'What do you mean warm-hearted – *filled with sex?*'

'No – this is not what *I* mean.'

Mr G.-J.: 'Miss Porter says the book is "a blood-chilling anatomy of the activities of the rutting season between two rather dull persons". Do you think that is a view one is entitled to hold?'

Mr Hough: 'Oh, anyone is entitled to hold any view. This one disposes of the argument that the book excites the sexual passions.'

(Again there is a slight ripple of laughter. Did the jury stir uneasily at academic levity?)

Mr G.-J.: 'Is this book "the feeble daydream of a dying man sitting under the umbrella pines indulging his sexual fantasies"?' (He puts the magazine down and looks at the witness.) '*Is this novel the feeble daydream of a dying man?*'

Mr Hough (very coldly): 'Lawrence died two years after publication.'

Mr Griffith-Jones dropped it, and started on another tack. 'Should a good book by a good writer repeat things again and again? This is a tiresome habit, is it not?'

'I don't agree with that. It is a technique

frequently employed . . . There is a great deal of repetition in the Bible—'

'Never mind the Bible. We are concerned with *this* book. Listen to this [reading]: "Connie went slowly home . . . Another self was alive in her, burning and molten and soft in her womb and bowels and with this self she adored him. She adored him till her knees were weak as she walked. In her womb and bowels she was flowing and alive now and vulnerable and helpless in adoration . . . " *Womb and bowels, womb and bowels*—' said Mr Griffith-Jones. 'Is that good writing? Or is it ludicrous?'

'Not to me.'

'We have two parts of her anatomy coupled together twice in three lines. Is that *expert* and *artistic* writing?'

'He is describing a woman in a highly emotional condition.'

The Judge joined in: 'Is it a piece of good English?'

Mr Hough: 'In context it is.'

Mr G.-J.: 'And in the last line of that page there is the phrase "bowels and womb" again. Is that writing of high *literary* merit?' And the prosecution pressed on, with hard persistence, pressed on and the scene took much longer, more beyond endurance than one could make it last with words on paper. It was a scene of wilful bullying, and like such scenes it was embarrassing to watch.

'I am asking you whether a work of high literary merit has that kind of repetition?'

Mr Hough: 'Knowing Lawrence, yes. It was his method. He was trying to describe—'

'Never mind what he was trying to describe. Is it good writing to repeat again and again "womb and bowels"?'

'Yes. It was his method.'

'It may well be his method. But has this kind of repetition any literary merit?'

'I would say so.'

Mr Griffith-Jones now read aloud another passage (page 204 of the Penguin edition). 'We have had two four-letter words appear repeatedly in twelve lines – is that a realistic conversation between a gamekeeper and a baronet's wife?'

'I don't think so,' said Mr Hough. 'I think as a passage this is a failure.'

Mr G.-J. (heavily): 'You grant me this much? In this book which is of such merit there is at least one passage which is a failure?'

'There are several,' said Mr Hough.

Mr G.-J. (reading a paragraph, p. 232): 'As a *literary critic* and an *expert*, do you regard this as good writing to repeat that offensive word three times?'

'I think in this case it is.'

Mr Griffith-Jones read the letter which is the finale of the novel. He read the passage of it that begins, 'So I love chastity now . . . ' He read it very badly, not on purpose, but like a man who reads a foreign language, a man who cannot see. The effect was unexpected. The power and beauty of Lawrence's writing carried. Up in the gallery, on the court benches, in the jury box, people were sitting absolutely quiet, listening, their hands still, listening, deeply moved.

Unaware, isolated, prosecuting counsel read on. He read the after-dinner conversation at Wragby. 'Does that conversation present an accurate picture of the way gentlemen of that class talk together on that kind of occasion with their hostess present?'

Mr Hough: 'I think it is quite convincing.'

Mr G.-J.: 'And the entire rest of the book, let's face it, is about sex? Even the old nurse – Mrs Bolton – is dragged in without any point at all so that Sir Clifford may feel her breasts?'

'There is very much point. This is most relevant . . . The decay of Clifford. Clifford is shown to have become like an unpleasant child.'

Mr G.-J.: 'Is there any particular literary or sociological advantage in having this described?'

'Yes, I think there is. These are representations of false and wrong sexual attitudes, and this is an important part of the book.'

'Where do the good attitudes come in?'

'Well, in the relationship between Connie and Mellors, who really loved one another.'

The judge raised an eyebrow. Mr Hough repeated his answer.

Mr G.-J.: 'Are you an expert on good sexual relationships?'

Mr Hough (calmly): 'I do not share the sexual ethics of D.H.L., I was never a disciple of his doctrine, but I think it is important and should be clearly stated.'

'Listen to this,' said Mr Griffith-Jones, ' "Lift up your heads O ye gates, that the King of glory may come in." We have looked up the correct quotation which is, "Lift up your heads O ye gates; and be ye lift up, ye ever-lasting doors; and the King of glory *shall* come in." Do you not think that if – in a book of literary merit – he is quoting from the Twenty-Fourth Psalm, he might look it up?'

Mr Hough: 'Oh, no. Writers often misquote. And in this case it is the gamekeeper who is speaking—'

'Do you think that the inclusion of the words from the Scriptures adds literary merit to the book?'

Here Mr Hough allowed himself once more to be flippant. 'I think it is the only sentence of this passage that *has* any literary merit.'

The second witness called turned out to be one of the most effective and impressive witnesses of the whole case. One saw climbing onto the witness stand a woman of homely appearance with a pleasant, open face, the kind of person one is apt to think jury members would welcome as a forthright and respected aunt; and indeed some of them were lifting trusting faces at her entrance. She was Helen Gardner.

'And are you,' said Mr Gardiner QC, 'the Reader in Renaissance English Literature at Oxford University? The author of books on T. S. Eliot, John Donne, and the Metaphysical Poets? A member of the Radio Critics' Panel?'

Miss Gardner said she was all these things.

'It has been said,' Mr Gardiner asked her, 'that

the four-letter words form the whole subject matter of the prosecution, and that one word occurred thirty times?'

Miss Gardner stood up there unruffled. It is not at all easy to come out well in that witness-box. It is very hard to lie successfully about a point of fact; it is impossible to get away with an opinion not sincerely held. You stand up there, very much exposed, all the eyes are on you; the jury, the bench, the two counsel are ready to pounce, to twist, to fling your words back at you. And at the end it all depends not on what you know and the ability to express it, not on courage and unflappability – though they all count – but on *what you are*. It shows. And that was why in this case nearly all those witnesses scored so heavily. They had come (at their own expense and risk) because they felt it their duty to do so; they were people of patent honesty and honour, people of splendid goodwill . . . and, of course, considerable abilities.

So Miss Gardner stood there and shone with goodness and integrity. She captured the hearts of the public gallery (many hardened murder-trial queuers among them), she may have captured the jury . . . 'I do not think words are brutal or disgusting in themselves,' she said; 'they are brutal if used in such a sense or context. The very fact that this word is used so frequently in this book means that with every use the original shock is diminished. By the time one has read the last page one feels that Lawrence has gone far to redeem this word.'

Mr Gardiner: 'What do you gather was Lawrence's original intention?'

'To make us feel that the sexual act is not shameful and the word used in its original sense is not shameful either,' she said with complete simplicity. 'Those passages succeed in doing something extraordinarily difficult, and very few writers have attempted with such courage and vision to put into verbal media experiences that are difficult to verbalise.'

'Do you feel any embarrassment in discussing this book in a mixed class?'

'Good gracious no,' said Miss Gardner.

'What, in your view, is the theme?'

'I think Lawrence felt very deeply the degrading conditions in which many people lived without beauty or joy and in slavery to what he calls, from William James, the Bitch Goddess Success, and he thought the most fundamental wrong was in the relationship between men and women – in sex; he thought through a better relationship there the whole of society might be revivified. Padding? *Oh, no!* It is a remarkable though not wholly successful novel, and though it doesn't rank with the greatest of Lawrence's work, I think certain passages are amongst his greatest. The ride through Derby-shire – the narrative of Mrs Bolton – oh, Mrs Bolton – a character worthy of Dickens.'

Mr Griffith-Jones had no questions. The pro-secution did not choose to cross-examine.

The next witness was Joan Bennett, the Cam-bridge don and critic (*George Eliot*, *The Victorian Novel*, etc.). She looked like a distinguished intellectual, in fact rather like Janet Flanner. She had a tendency to answer quickly, and then to qualify. Mr Griffith-Jones kept his eye on her.

Lawrence's view, she said, was that the physical life was of great importance; many people lived poor emasculated lives, they only lived with one half of themselves; Lawrence dealt with sex seriously, very seriously . . . Promiscuous inter-course was shown as unsatisfactory, giving no fulfilment or joy, as being rather disgusting . . . He thought that marriage was a complete relation-ship, marriage, not quite in the legal sense, but a union between two people for a lifetime was of the highest importance, of almost sacred importance—

'What did you say?' said the Judge. '*Of almost sacred importance*.' He wrote it down.

Mr Gardiner: 'And have you got one son, three daughters and eight grandchildren?'

'I have,' said Mrs Bennett.

Mr Griffith-Jones was ready for her. 'Does not this book show a picture of a woman who has sexual relationships with people who are not her husband?'

'Yes.'

'Does this adulterous intercourse show a regard for marriage as it is generally understood by the average reader?'

'What average reader?' asked Mrs Bennett, faithful to precision. 'If you mean an intelligent child—'

Mr G.-J.: 'If you *can* come down to our humbler level from your academic heights will you answer my question – does this book show regard for marriage?'

'In what sense do you mean marriage?'

The Judge leaned toward her: 'Lawful wedlock, madam!'

Mrs Bennett said bravely, though in not too sure a voice, 'Lawrence believed it can be – as I think the law allows – broken in certain conditions.'

Down swooped Mr Griffith-Jones: 'Is not that precisely what Lawrence himself did? He ran off with somebody else's wife, did he not? Did he not?'

MR GARDINER's re-examination consisted of one question.

'Did D. H. Lawrence's one and only marriage last his lifetime?'

'It did,' said Mrs Bennett.

'I call,' said Mr Gardiner, 'Dame Rebecca West.'

Dame Rebecca went into that box and said her say. There was no prodding *her* into the question-and-answer shafts. She made the points she found necessary to make, she made them in her own way and she made them well, and that was that.

The story of Lady Chatterley, she said, was designed as an allegory; the baronet and his impotence were a symbol of the impotent culture of our time which had become sterile and un-helpful to man's deepest needs, and the love affair with the gamekeeper was a return of the soul to a more intense life. Lawrence was not a fanciful writer; he knew he was writing about something *quite real* – he saw that in every country in the world there were populations who had lost touch with life and who could be exploited. All the time he was governed by this fear that something was going to happen – fascism, nazism – something that did happen in the shape of the war . . .

Of course one could find individual passages which appeared to have no literary merit. By this time Dame Rebecca was addressing the court and jury as she might some fairly alert committee. 'But the same is true of Shakespeare and Wordsworth, they all have some terrible lines. *Lady Chatterley* is full of sentences any child could make a fool of. You see, Lawrence was a man without a background of formal education and he also had one great defect which impairs this book, he had absolutely no sense of humour. And a lot of the scenes are, I think, ludicrous. But in spite of the ugly things, the ugly words, it is still a good book.'

Witnesses of sufficient eminence, or who have shown a deal of character, were not likely to be cross-examined. They might boomerang. Dame Rebecca was not questioned; the prosecution left well enough alone.

*

MR GARDINER said, 'I am calling the Bishop of Woolwich!'

This was the moment of thrill for the regular crime reporters, who now made a dash for their telephones. The Bishop looked delightful, like a well-groomed and angelic poet, and he wore his pectoral cross and violet silk cloth with a romantic air. He admitted to being Dr John Arthur Thomas Robinson, the father of four children, the author of several works on the New Testament, and to having long experience in teaching and ministering to university students. He had read *Lady Chatterley's Lover* in the summer.

He was cut short by Mr Griffith-Jones: 'I submit that the Bishop cannot be heard – his qualifications do not entitle him to give evidence about the book's literary merit.'

Mr Gardiner said the Bishop had come to give evidence on its ethical merits.

Mr G.-J.: 'Ethical merits are not mentioned in the Obscene Publications Act.'

Mr Gardiner: 'My Lord, the Act mentions art or learning or other objects of general concern.'

The Judge: 'I agree with you, ethics must be considered an object of general concern.'

So the Bishop was allowed to proceed.

'Clearly,' he said, 'Lawrence did not have a Christian valuation of sex, and the kind of relationships depicted in the book are not necessarily of the kind I should regard as ideal. But what Lawrence is trying to do, I think, is to portray the sex relationship as something sacred . . . I might quote Archbishop Temple: "Christians do not make jokes about sex for the same reason they do not make jokes about Holy Communion, not because it is sordid but because it is sacred." I think Lawrence tried to portray this relation in the real sense as an act of holy communion, in a lower case. For him flesh was sacramental . . . '

The Judge took it down ostentatiously.

'Lawrence's descriptions of sexual relationships cannot be taken out of the context of his whole quite astonishing sensitivity to the beauty and value of all organic relationships. Some of the descriptions of nature in the books seem to me extraordinarily beautiful, and to portray an attitude to the whole organic world in which he saw sex as the culmination.'

Mr Gardiner: 'Can you make a distinction between the book as it is, and as it would be with the sexual passages left out?'

The Bishop: 'I think the effect of that would be

41

to suggest that what Lawrence was doing was something sordid and could be put before the public only if the passages about sex were eliminated. I think that is a false view. I think neither in intention nor in effect is this book depraving.'

'It has been said that it puts promiscuous and adulterous intercourse on a pedestal.'

'That seems a distorted view. In the last pages there is a tremendous and most moving advocacy of chastity: "How can men want wearisomely to philander?" '

The Bishop's cross-examination took place after the luncheon adjournment. By that time on that day one of the unusual features of this trial had become more distinct, and that was the invasion of the professional sanctity of the court by the outer world. The Old Bailey is very much a place of its own, a highly specialised place where (apart from the occasional sensational trial) humdrum, brutal, shabby crime is dealt with day after day, in a steady, drab, conscientious grind. The prisoner sits in the dock, the contests are fought between teams of professionals and their attendants. Of course, there are other people in court, but they don't count. They are there because they must: if the accused has partisans they are helpless people, frightened, involved; his wretched wife perhaps in a back row, a humbled father; or they are there out of some unengaged curiosity, or to do a job, law pupils, the regular crime reporters, a pack of Pavlov dogs sitting in their pew waiting for their cues of sex and violence. This, then, was one of the rare occasions when the court was packed with outside people of conscience, heart and mind, people who were passionately concerned about the outcome, and who were not wholly – at least outside the actual court – mute and powerless: writers, poets, educators, Lawrence enthusiasts, literary journalists, English, American, Canadian . . . The French, or members of other Latin nations, did not participate.

Mr Griffith-Jones started with this question to the Bishop: 'Do you tell us that this book is a valuable work on ethics?'

The Bishop answered that it had positive value from an ethical point of view.

'It is not a treatise on marriage, but Lawrence made it clear that he was not against marriage relationships—'

Mr G.-J.: 'I don't want to be offensive to you, but you are not here to make speeches. Just answer my questions. Are you asking the jury to accept this book as a valuable work on ethics?'

'I would not say it had an *instructional* value—'

'Is it a book Christians ought to read?'

The Judge: 'Does it portray the love of an immoral woman?'

The Bishop: 'It portrays the love of a woman in an immoral relationship, so far as adultery is an immoral relationship.'

By now Bench and prosecution were seen to have spun themselves into the old fallacy: a book dealing with immorality is an immoral book. It is neither law nor logic, but it is an easy web for juries to get lost in, and the Churchman at any rate was being shown as having tied himself into apparent knots.

'*Is* this a book Christians ought to read?' asked Mr Griffith-Jones.

'Yes, I think it is. And because—' But the Bishop was not allowed to explain; the prosecution stopped him in his tracks. And by evening the headlines proclaimed: Bishop's Defence of Lady C – Book All Christians Ought To Read.

'SIR WILLIAM EMRYS WILLIAMS!' A director of Penguin Books, Secretary-General of the Arts Council, knighted in 1955.

'Will you explain why you printed 200,000 copies of this book?'

'That is nothing out of the ordinary. An average first printing of a Penguin would be 40,000 to 50,000 copies, but for some books we print as many as 250,000.'

'Why did you not think of putting in rows of asterisks?'

Sir William: 'That would make it a dirty book.'

'What about dashes for the four-letter words?'

'That would make for unwholesomeness.'

'Do you think you could have sold a large number of copies of an *expurgated* edition?'

'Quite the same number.' (There is in fact such an expurgated edition published in Britain, and it sold nearly a quarter million copies in nine months last year.)

'PROFESSOR VIVIAN DE SOLA PINTO!' Professor of English at Nottingham University; perhaps one of the greatest D. H. Lawrence authorities living today.

Mr Griffith-Jones (cross-examining): 'Professor, just let me make sure what your ideas of beauty are?' He reads.

Professor Pinto: 'An able piece of realism.'

Mr Griffith-Jones (furiously): 'Cunt! Cunt! Cunt! Cunt! Fuck! Fuck! Fuck! Fuck!'

'The Reverend A. S. Hopkinson!' Vicar of St Catherine Cree, London; General Director of Industrial Christian Fellowship; Anglican Adviser to Associated Television.

' . . . A study in compassion . . . A book of moral purpose.' ('A book of?' said the Judge.) ' . . . All comes from God, thus sex comes from God; it is utterly wrong to link sex with sin. The words? The words are about activities that are an essential part of human life; it would be a mistake to replace them with blanks . . . Yes, I would like my children to read it, I should like them to discuss it with me and their mother.'

The Judge asked: 'You have no objection to your children reading this book?'

'Only one of them has, to my knowledge,' said the clergyman, 'and he found it rather dull.'

Mr Griffith-Jones: 'As a minister of the Church, you would have the highest opinion of the marriage vows?'

'Yes.'

'Would you not agree that this was a book about a man and a woman who have little regard for the marriage vow at all?'

'No.'

Mr G.-J.: 'I am sure you do not hold the view that we can throw our marriage bond overboard?'

'No, I do not.'

'That is what this woman is doing! That is what this whole book is about – she throws her marriage bond overboard in order to get sexual satisfaction. That is what this book teaches.'

'With respect, I should say that the marriage goes wrong, and afterwards she takes the wrong course.'

Mr G.-J.: 'None of you experts in this case is able to say Yes or No to any question! Listen to this, "Lift up your heads O ye gates . . . " ' He read the whole Psalm passage again. 'Is that shocking? Blasphemous?'

'That was not the author's intention.'

'We are not concerned with the author's intention. Answer my question, will you? Were you shocked to find a Psalm in such a passage?'

'I did not recognise the Psalm.'

'MR ST JOHN-STEVAS!' MA Oxford and Cambridge; PhD Columbia; LLD Yale; Academic Lawyer and Qualified Barrister; author of *Obscenity and the Law*; legal adviser to the Committee which sponsored the Obscene Publications Bill; a Roman Catholic; student of Moral Theology; and still a very young man.

He said he would put Lawrence among the great literary moralists of our literature.

'Lawrence was essentially concerned to purge, cleanse, reform. I have been horrified by the representation of him in some newspapers, in papers which I think he wouldn't have deigned to read!

'I have had the misfortune to have to read through a vast number of books of a pornographic and obscene nature, and I find it difficult to make comparisons with *Lady Chatterley*, so great is the gulf between them.'

Mr Hutchinson asked him if he found the book consistent with the tenets of his own faith.

Mr St John-Stevas said: Quite consistent. Of course Lawrence was neither a Christian nor a Catholic, but one could say he was a writer essentially in the Catholic tradition. 'I mean by that the tradition that the sex instinct is good in itself, is implanted in man by God, is one of his greatest gifts. This tradition was opposed by the movement which started at the Reformation and has grown in Protestant minds that sex is something "which is wrong", which is essentially evil.'

'I call the Headmaster of Alleyns!' DSO; former Military Governor of Berlin (not cross-examined).

'I call the Master of the Temple!' Canon of Lincoln Cathedral (not cross-examined).

'Mr Roy Jenkins, MP!' (Not cross-examined.)

All that day, and the next day, and the next, that procession of defence witnesses went on, professors, editors, schoolmasters, critics, poets, clergymen of the Church of England, psychologists . . .

THERE CAME to many of us a most moving moment, when counsel called: 'Edward Morgan Forster!' And in came Mr E. M. Forster – alone – he had been sitting waiting on a bench in the hall the best part of the morning, waiting to be called. Now here he was, in a mackintosh, old only in years, looking very firm and calm.

The greatest living writer perhaps in the English language had come into this court, and of course there was no sign of recognition; that is not within the rules or spirit of the place. But Mr Jeremy Hutchinson, very likely seized by a desire to do something, chose the one gesture of favour or respect that can be made in a courtroom – he asked the judge if Mr E. M. Forster might be given a chair. His Lordship said: Certainly. But Mr Forster said, no, no, he didn't want one, he didn't want a chair. Then he spoke.

'I knew Lawrence quite well. In nineteen hundred and fifteen . . . ' And there came a sense of the past, and the years.

How would he place him in English literature, asked Mr Hutchinson.

'I would place him enormously high. The greatest imaginative writer of his generation . . . He is part of the great puritan stream of writers, Bunyan, Blake . . . Though that may seem a bit paradoxical at first sight. A preacher . . . '

But Mr Forster's passage was all too brief. Mr Griffith-Jones said he had no question, and Mr Forster was gone.

'I CALL SIR STANLEY UNWIN!'

'Miss C.V. Wedgwood!'

'Mr Walter Allen!' Novelist and literary critic.

'In your professional capacity, how many novels do you read a year?'

'Up to two hundred.'

'How would you describe *Lady Chatterley's Lover*?'

Walter Allen: 'A tract and the work of a genius.'

'Miss Sarah Beryl Jones!' Classics Mistress and Senior Librarian at Keighley Grammar School. A little grey-haired woman, who speaks her own form of oath.

The Judge: 'What did you say?'

Miss Jones (bright and fussy): 'The whole truth as far as I am able to speak it.' She is made to eat those words.

Mr Gardiner: 'Do girls grow up earlier now than they used to?'

Miss Jones: 'In my experience, yes.'

'Is there a good deal of literature available to them on sexual matters?'

'There are technical works, and there are what you might call dirty books.'

'How far do girls understand the four-letter words?'

Miss Jones: 'I have inquired of a number of girls – after they left school – and most of them have been acquainted with them since the age of ten.'

'Has *Lady Chatterley's Lover* any educational value?'

'Considerable value, if taken at the right age, which is normally after seventeen, because it deals honestly and openly with problems of sex which are very real to the girls themselves. Girls are very good at knowing what is good for them. Girls read what they want to read and they don't read what they don't want to read.'

'Miss Ann Scott-James!' A most smartly dressed young woman.

Mr Griffith-Jones rises at once to object.

'I understand you are the editor of a Ladies' Page?'

Miss Scott-James: 'Not a Ladies' Page. It hasn't been called that since 1912. A Woman's Page.'

'Do you claim any particular qualification to be a literary expert?'

'Of a popular kind. And I was a classical scholar at Oxford.' She adds disarmingly, 'It's not a negligible qualification.'

Mr G.-J.: 'Does that make you a literary expert?'

'I was brought up in a very literary family. My father—' But Miss Scott-James is whisked out of the box.

'Mr Stephen Potter!'

'When I read the book again, I was surprised by its power! . . . And the words only shock the eye, and that soon goes because they do not shock the brain. I think what D.H.L. was trying to do was something very difficult and courageous, he was trying to take these words out of the context of the lavatory wall.'

'Dr Clifford James Hemming!' Writer, lecturer, educational psychologist.

'Young people,' he said, 'reading *Lady Chatterley* might find themselves for the first time confronted with a concept of sex which includes compassion and tenderness.

'Young people nowadays are subject to constant insinuation of shallow and corrupting values . . . Books and papers tell the young girl that if she has the right proportions, wears the right clothes, uses the right cosmetics, she will become irresistible to men, and that this is the supreme achievement of women, to become irresistible to men. And as far as the men are concerned, it is suggested that to have a pretty woman in your arms is the supreme thrill of life, and to seduce a woman is manful in yourself and something to envy in others. The contents of *Lady Chatterley* are an antidote. They show all that makes sex human . . . '

Mr Gardiner: 'Are the detailed descriptions justified? Are they of any sociological value?'

'Oh, yes,' said Dr Hemming. 'It is now recognised

that for young people to grow up and marry with brutish and ashamed attitudes is most harmful. The rejection of our bodies can lead to mental ill health. This book would act as a positive antidote to those promiscuous and dehumanising influences.'

There was no doubt that the prosecution and the Bench were flabbergasted to be hearing what they heard. The views of apparently respectable professional men and women . . . Chaos, it must have seemed to Mr Justice Byrne, had come again.

Mr Griffith-Jones, in cross-examination, asked, not unexpectedly: 'Let us see what amounts to an antidote.' And he began his now-familiar tone-deaf reading. 'Is *that* an antidote to promiscuous sex among young people?'

Dr Hemming: 'Yes.'

'That was a description of what was happening just before the act of intercourse?'

'Yes.'

'That was promiscuous intercourse by Lady Chatterley?'

Dr Hemming: 'Yes, but it is quite different from the street-corner promiscuity which is one of our problems today.'

Mr G.-J.: 'I was not limiting my meaning to

street corners. Is there anything to suggest that *she* wouldn't have gone on and on, from man to man, until she found someone who satisfied her?'

Dr Hemming: 'That is a conjectural question. I do not believe she would have led that kind of life.'

As one can see, Constance Chatterley had ceased to be a character of fiction. To the defence she was poor Connie; to the other side, Lady Chatterley, a traitor to her class, a shocking example, and the guilty party to a divorce action of the most undesirable nature.

Mr G.-J.: 'Here we have another one of the bouts. Listen.' (He reads.) 'Does that strengthen the antidote much, does it?'

Dr Hemming: 'I don't see why not.'

' "As he found her", what do you think these words mean?'

'Getting into closer intimacy.'

Mr G.-J.: 'What do you mean?'

'What Lawrence means.'

'What do *you* mean by that?'

'A continuation of the physical act of love.'

Mr G.-J.: 'What do you mean by that? I shall go on asking you until you tell us in plain good English words what you think that means!'

Dr Hemming: 'He was caressing her.'

'Where?'

'It doesn't say.'

'Where do you think?'

No answer.

'*Where?*'

And so it went on.

Sometime later, a witness, an Oxford don, read D.H.L.'s own comment. ' "It's the one thing they won't let you be, straight and open in your sex. You can be as dirty as you like. In fact, the more dirt you do on sex the better they like it. But if you believe in your own sex and won't have it done dirt to, they down you. It's the one insane taboo left – sex as a natural and vital thing." '

TO UNDERSTAND the conduct of the prosecution case, it may perhaps be well to bear several rather contradictory things in mind. One: prosecuting counsel acts as an advocate; it is his job to present one side, and to present it strongly, to the best of his abilities. This, however, is somewhat weakened by the concurrent principle by which the prosecution is held to present all the facts fairly and not to press for a conviction *per se*; and so it can be said that counsel's job is not to press a case beyond its merits.

Two: a criminal trial is the trial of an issue of fact; was this act committed, and was it committed in such and such a way, yes or no? Did this man stab his wife, did that man steal a load of cheeses? It is not a matter of opinion, it is a matter of facts – the knife, the prints, the eyewitness, the alibi. And this is where the prosecution here, and the whole legal machinery, ran into trouble. They were dealing with something pressed into a Procrustean framework devised for something else; they were dealing with what was in reality an issue of judgement or opinion by a procedure created for the pinning down of fact.

Obscenity, unlike murder and theft, is not self-evident fact; it involves, in (US) Judge Bryan's words, 'questions of constitutional judgment of the most sensitive and delicate kind'; it involves definitions, definitions depending on – relative and changeable – community standards, on private feelings, on opinions. And below the standards, the feelings and opinions, lie the powers of what are perhaps our deepest and most irrational taboos. In regard to sex, and even more so in regard to certain words, England is still Disraeli's Two Nations, and the thought barrier between them is complete.

And so, three: in a true issue of fact, counsel's feelings or opinions are of no account and must never be expressed. In this case counsel did express feelings and opinions. For one thing, because he could hardly help doing so in the context. But they also were, and this was crystal clear to everyone present, his own feelings and opinions, and he believed in them to the exclusion of anybody else's. He, like the witnesses, was the man he was, and that comprised, evidently, that he had never in his life been conditioned to regard with respect any modern classic in the realm of purely imaginative writing. Confronted with a very difficult one, he displayed his natural reactions.

And it must be for something of all these three considerations that the cross-examinations were so indignant, so ineffective and so very much beside the point.

'The Dean of the Faculty of Arts at Liverpool University!'

'The Editor of the *Manchester Guardian*!'

'The Provost of King's!'

'Sir Allen Lane!' Founder of Penguin Books.

'Mr C. Day Lewis!'

'The Former Precentor of Birmingham Cathedral!' and Director of Religious Education.

' . . . By reading it, young people will be helped to grow up as mature and responsible people . . . '

The prosecution made a point of cross-examining nearly all the clergy. Their position was most vulnerable. (In fact, the Bishop of Woolwich was rebuked by the Archbishop of Canterbury after the trial.)

Mr Griffith-Jones: 'Is there anything to suggest that marriage is sacred and inviolable?'

'It is a novel.'

Mr Griffith-Jones repeats the question.

'I think it is taken for granted.'

'Let us see. Mellors, the gamekeeper, did not regard marriage as sacred and inviolable?'

'He was very much attracted by Lady Chatterley.'

'Of course he was. Everybody who commits adultery is very much attracted by the man or woman with whom he does it. Just answer my question please.'

The Judge: 'Does the book really deal with anything other than adultery?'

'Mr John Connell!' the writer and critic.

'I disagree utterly and totally about all those suggestions about indulgence and promiscuity and padding. The book is concerned with two intertwined themes in human life and English society –

sex and class. And it deals with a tragic situation.'

Mr Hutchinson: 'What about an expurgated edition?'

Mr Connell: 'I was unfortunate enough to be sent one for review the other day. I found it: a) trivial, b) furtive, c) obscene.'

A reader, having reached this stage, may well feel that the portents now were for acquittal. All those witnesses, the sheer weight of numbers must have left their mark. Had they? We were far from certain. The lawyers and defendants were only faintly hopeful. A hung jury, perhaps. The American journalists present looked at us with pity. The more enlightened court decision of their country had not been allowed to be heard in evidence.

'Do you know,' Mr Gardiner had asked, 'of any civilised country where this book cannot be bought except in Lawrence's own Common-wealth?' Mr Griffith-Jones had objected, 'What happens in other countries is not relevant,' he said. Mr Gardiner put forward that it would be evidence of literary value. 'I'm against that,' had said Mr Justice Byrne.

The regular reporters told one with satisfied cynicism, 'They won't get away with it – no British jury will swallow those words.' So one went on staring at this British jury. Most of them looked like pleasant people. The women seemed at their ease. There were two of them besides the twelfth juror; one very pretty young woman with a gentle face – ought one to pin hopes on her? – and one middle-aged, more of the housewife type. The second day she had appeared without a hat. A favourable sign? One man often dozed. Another looked worried. Another sullen. The foreman, the twelfth juror and one or two of the men laughed and talked as they walked through the vestibule, a most unprecedented thing.

IF THE CASE had any turning point at all, it must have been the exchange with the most quietly and fervently assured (as well as one of the most brilliantly intelligent) of the witnesses, Richard Hoggart, on Day Three. Mr Hoggart, Senior Lecturer in English at Leicester University, is a young man from the Midlands, dark and short, born, like Lawrence himself, into the coal-mining working class. He started his education at an elementary school.

He had called *Lady Chatterley* a highly virtuous, if not a puritanical book, and Mr Hutchinson had invited him to enlarge on that.

'I was thinking of the whole movement of the book, of Lawrence's enormous insistence on arriving at relationships of integrity. I was struck on re-reading it to realise how much of it is contemporary; it tells us a great deal about our society at a level which we do not usually probe, and with an insight which we do not usually attain . . . It makes you consider your relationship to society, it teaches you to question your place and your being . . . '

Mr Hutchinson: 'It has been suggested that the only variations in the sexual descriptions lay in where they took place.'

'A gross misreading,' said Mr Hoggart firmly. 'I don't mean highbrow reading. I mean an honest reading.'

Mr Hutchinson asked him about repetition of words.

'Indeed, yes. It's one of Lawrence's characteristics, and one he uses to great effect. He hammered home and almost recreated words. Shakespeare repeated "nothing" five times in one passage.'

Mr Hutchinson asked if the four-letter words were genuine and necessary.

No one who saw him on that morning will

ever forget Richard Hoggart, how he stood up there talking in his serious, clear-minded, communicating way. And now he uttered the words we had so far only heard from the lips of the prosecution.

'They are totally characteristic of many people,' he said, 'and I would like to say not only working-class people, because that would be wrong. They are used very freely indeed, far more freely than many of us know. Fifty yards from this court this morning, I heard a man say that word three times as I passed him, one, two, three, I heard him. He must have been very angry.

'These are common words; if you work on a building site, as I have done, you will hear them frequently. But the man I heard this morning and the men on the building site use this word as a word of contempt, and one of the most horrifying things to Lawrence was that the word used for sex has become a term of violent abuse, and has totally lost its meaning. He wanted to re-establish the proper meaning of it.

'When I first read it, the first effect was one of some shock, obviously because it is not used in polite literature. But as one read, one found the word losing that shock. We have no word in English which is not either an abstraction or has become an evasive euphemism for this act; we are constantly running away from it or dissolving into dots. I realised that it is we who are wrong. Lawrence was wanting to show what one does in the most simple, neutral way . . . Just like that, with no snigger or dirt. That is what one does.'

Mr Griffith-Jones rose to cross-examine. And he underestimated Mr Hoggart's effectiveness, virtue and strength; the passage that followed was the prosecution's biggest moral defeat in the case.

Mr Griffith-Jones: 'You described this as a puritanical book. Is that your genuine and considered view?'

'Yes.'

Mr G.-J. (with gentlemanly superiority): 'I think I must have lived my life under a mis-apprehension of the word "puritanical". Will you help me?'

Mr Hoggart (earnest and friendly): 'Yes, I will. Many people do live their lives under a mis-apprehension of the meaning of puritanical. In Britain, and for a long time, the word has pretended to mean somebody who is against anything which is pleasurable, particularly sex, but the proper meaning of it to an historian is somebody who belongs to the tradition of British puritanism, and the main weight of that is an intense sense of responsibility for one's conscience. In that sense the book is puritanical.'

Mr Griffith-Jones said: 'I am obliged to you for the lecture.' (He reads a sexual passage.) 'Is that puritanical?'

Mr Hoggart: 'Yes. Heavy with conscience.'

'I am not asking you if it is heavy with conscience. I am asking you if it is puritanical.'

'Yes. It is one of the side issues of puritanism.'

Mr G.-J. (reading a passage from the Michaelis episode): 'Puritanical?'

'Yes – puritanical, poignant, tender, moving, and about two people who have no proper relationship.'

Mr G.-J.: 'I should have thought that could be answered without a lecture. This is the Old Bailey, and not [with thin distaste] *Leicester* University.'

A further passage.

Mr G.-J.: 'That is about all there is to keep those two connected? It was done purely for the satisfaction of her sexual lust, wasn't it?'

Mr Hoggart: 'No, it was done because she is lonely and lost, and she feels through the sexual act she may feel less lonely and lost.'

Mr Justice Byrne: 'It is just an immoral relationship between a man and a woman?'

Mr Hoggart: 'Yes.' (Suddenly, eagerly.) 'In Milton, in *Paradise Lost*, there is a great passage in which Adam and Eve come together in this way . . . Highly sensual . . . '

Mr Griffith-Jones then read that extraordinary page about the source of life. Again he read as though it were some foreign text; again the court sat rapt. ' "The weight of a man's balls" – puritanical?'

'Yes, it is puritanical in its reverence.'

'Reverence for what?' screamed Mr Griffith-Jones. '*The balls?*'

'Indeed, yes,' said Mr Hoggart gently.

AT THE END of Day Four, Mr Gardiner said that, although they still had thirty-six witnesses in reserve, of 'the same sort of character and standing', the defence would call only one more. The prosecution now had the right to call witnesses in rebuttal, but Mr Griffith-Jones said he did not propose to call any evidence. And so the case had reached the stage of the final speeches. The speech for the defence and the speech for the prosecution were two speeches made from two different levels, addressed to two kinds of people. Only one question remained: Which kind was the jury?

Mr Gardiner rose to speak the next morning. His manner was quiet though firm, and he anticipated a good many prosecution points.

'It might be suggested,' he told the jury, 'that you should ignore the evidence given by the witnesses on the ground that it was given by professors of literature, by people who are living rarefied lives and are not really in touch with ordinary people. And indeed, no higher class of experts could have been called on any similar occasion.' Now the most important single fact here was that Parliament had expressly provided that evidence may be called both by the defence and by the prosecution; yet when the prosecution's turn came to call evidence, they called none at all. 'Not one single witness has been found to say anything against Lawrence or this book; we have only got to go by what Mr Griffith-Jones said himself when opening the case.

' . . . Hardly any question has been put to witnesses [by the prosecution] about the book as a whole. The technique has been that used before the new Act: to read out a particular passage and to say, is that moral?

' . . . This is a book about human beings, about real people, and I protest at the statements that have been made about the characters, about Constance, as though she were a sort of nympho-maniac. When it is said that this is just a book about adultery, one wonders how there can be things which people cannot see? I suppose some-where there may be a mind which would describe *Antony and Cleopatra* as a play about adultery, the story of a sex-starved Roman soldier copulating with an Egyptian queen.

'As a book published at 3/6, *Lady Chatterley* will be available to the general public and it may well be said that everyone will rush to buy it. This is always the effect of a wrong prosecution.

'Witnesses have been asked if it was a book they would like their wife or servant to read. This may have been consciously or unconsciously an echo of the Bench of years ago: "It would never do to let the members of the working class read this." I don't want to upset the prosecution by suggesting there are a certain number of people who do not have servants. This whole attitude is one Penguin Books was formed to fight against. It is the attitude that it is all right to publish a special edition at five or ten guineas, but quite wrong to let people who are less well-off read what those other people read. Is not everyone, whether their income is ten pounds or twenty pounds a week, equally interested in the society in which we live? In the problems of our relationships, including sexual relationships?

' . . . It would be very easy to say to you for counsel for the prosecution, "You and I are ordinary chaps, don't you bother about those experts – they don't really know what goes on in the world at all." Lawrence, members of the jury, was a man of the people. There are students of literature in all walks of life . . . If it is right that the book should be read, it should be available to the man working in a factory as it is to the teacher working in a school.

' . . . In England we have before banned books by Hardy, G. B. Shaw, Ibsen, Wilde, Joyce, and even Epstein's statues. But is Lawrence to be always confined to dirty bookshops? This would be the greatest irony in literary history.

' . . . A book is not obscene merely because part of its subject matter is a relationship between people who are not married, or who are married to someone else. If that were so, ninety per cent of English literature is obscene.

' . . . Can it be seriously suggested that anyone's character will be changed by reading words that they already know?

'I submit that the defence has shown on balance of probabilities that it is for the public good that this book should be generally available . . . If this is not a book to which the Section of the new Act applies, then it is difficult to conceive of any book by such an author to which it can apply.

'We are a country known throughout the world for our literature and our democratic institutions. It is strange indeed that this is the only country where this Englishman's work cannot be read. Lawrence lived and died suffering from the public opinion, caused by the banning of this book, that he had written a piece of pure pornography. For the first time this case has enabled the book to be dragged out into the light of day. The slur was never justified. All the time the book was a passionate and sincere work of a moralist who believed he had a message for us in the society in which we live. Whether we agree with what he had in view or not, is it not time we rescued Lawrence's name from the quite unjust reputation and allowed our people – his people – to judge for themselves? I leave Lawrence's reputation and the reputation of Penguin Books with confidence in your hands.'

Mr Griffith-Jones' speech followed.

'This is a case of immense importance, and its effects will go far beyond the actual question which the jury has to decide.

' . . . It has been emphasised that you have heard no witnesses called by the prosecution. It may sound a good point to reiterate again and again, but it is an empty point, and not the kind of argument on which you are to decide the case. The law restricts me to calling evidence only as to the literary, artistic and other merits of the book. As to the merit of the book as literature, I have from the first conceded that Lawrence was a great writer. These are matters upon which the prosecution never sought to argue, and upon which it would have been wholly irrelevant and redundant for me to call evidence. On whether the book is of educational or sociological merit, I am happy to leave that aspect to the book itself. I cannot believe that you, or any other jury, would wish evidence to be called simply to hear these words: This book is not a great educational document, nor is it of great sociological value.

'Members of the jury, there are standards, are

there not? There must be standards which we are to maintain, standards, of morality, language and conduct, which are essential to the well-being of our society. They must be instilled in all of us, and at the earliest possible age, standards of respect for the conventions, for the kind of conduct society approves, for other people's feelings, and there must be instilled in all of us standards of restraint.

'You have only to read your papers and see day by day the results of unbridled sex . . . It is all for lack of standards, lack of restraint, lack of mental and moral discipline . . .

' . . . It is true, as Mr Gardiner has anticipated, that I would urge upon you that you alone will have to decide, and not the various witnesses whose views you have heard. You will not be browbeaten by these witnesses, you will judge the case as ordinary men and women, with your feet firmly planted on the ground. Were the views you have heard from those most eminent and academic ladies and gentlemen really of so much value as the views which *you* – without perhaps the eminence and the academic learning – possess yourselves? I do not question the integrity and sincerity of those witnesses, but suggest that they all have got a bee in their bonnet about this book . . .

'When one sees some of them launching themselves at the first opportunity, at the first question, into a sermon or a lecture – according to their vocation – one cannot help feeling that, sincerely and honestly as they feel, they feel in such a way that common sense perhaps has gone by the board.

'One witness said that sex was treated "on a holy basis". Can that be a realistic view? Is that a way a boy leaving school would read it? The Bishop of Woolwich went one better and called it something as sacred as an Act of Holy Communion. Do you think that is the way girls working in a factory will read the book in their luncheon break? Or does it put the Lord Bishop wholly out of touch with the large percentage of the people who will buy this book at 3/6?

'A book of moral purpose, the Reverend Hopkinson has said. *What* moral purpose do *you* read into the book?

'I suggest that Miss [*sic*] Rebecca West is capable of reading what she said into the book, but is that typical of the effect that book will have on the average reader? Are they going to see an allegory in it? Is the baronet and his impotence going to be read by them as a symbol? One wonders whether one is talking in the same language . . .

'Members of the jury, is there any moral teaching in the book at all? How can there be when right until the end, when they decide to get their respective divorces, not a single word is spoken between them during their thirteen bouts, other than sex? All they have done before they decide to run away with each other is to copulate thirteen times . . .

'It has been suggested that the shock of using the foul words wore off as one got used to it. Is that not a terrible thing if we forget the shock of using this language?'

And here Mr Griffith-Jones took up the book once more. Once more he read. He read the Psalm passage again. 'Do you know *who* the King of glory is? Do you?' He read another. 'Here we come to a little striptease . . . ' He read again the last letter; he read, for the first time, two pages of Connie's last night with Mellors before she leaves for Venice.

He shut the book. 'You will have to go some way in the Charing Cross Road, in the back streets of Paris, or even Port Saïd, to find a description that is as lurid as that one.

'It is for the jury to decide this case, and not for the so-called experts. This book has to be read not as bishops and lecturers read it, but as ordinary men and women read it, people without any literary or academic qualifications. Do you think, as I submit, that its effect on the average person must be to deprave, to lead them into false conceptions, to lower their general standard of thought, conduct and decency, and must be the opposite of encouraging that restraint in sexual matters which is so all-important in present times? This is what you must ask yourselves. And if you decide that it has a tendency to deprave, then you have to ask yourselves what public good is being done by this book to outweigh the harm. Is there such a public need in the interest of public good for the publication of this document?

'There can be but one answer.'

There was still the Judge. Juries are apt to look up to the Judge, and to look at him to clarify their minds. Mr Justice Byrne began his summing-up on the afternoon of Day Five and continued on Day Six. He began: 'In these days the world seems to be full of experts. There is no subject you can think of where there is not to be found an expert who will be able to deal, or says he will be able to deal, with the situation. But the criminal law is based on a view that a jury is responsible for the facts and not the experts.'

The Judge's voice was discreet in tone, polite and quietly persuasive. He spoke for two and a half hours all in all, and here are some extracts from what he said.

'There is no intent to deprave necessary to be proved in order that this offence should be committed. The intention is quite irrelevant.

' . . . This book is to be put upon the market at 3/6 a copy, which is by no means an excessive price in these days when there are not only high wages, but high pocket money . . . Once a book gets into circulation, it does not spend its time in the rarefied atmosphere of some academic institution; it finds its way into the bookshops and onto the bookstalls and into the public libraries where it is available to all and sundry to read.

' . . . The book has been said to be a moral tract, a virtuous and puritanical production, and a book that Christians ought to read. What do *you* think about that?

'Is it right to say that the story is one of a woman who first of all before she was married had sexual intercourse, and then after marriage when her husband had met with disaster in the war, and became confined to a wheelchair, she was living with her husband in this dreary place, Wragby, and committed adultery on two occasions with somebody called Michaelis, while her husband was downstairs in the same house. After that she proceeded to have adulterous intercourse with her husband's gamekeeper. And that is described, you may think – is it or is it not? – in the most lurid way, and the whole sensuality and passion of the various occasions is fully and completely described.

' . . . You will have to consider the tendency that this book will have on the moral outlook of people who buy it, people possibly without any knowledge of Lawrence, or of literature, and people perhaps quite young, the youth of the country.

' . . . If you are satisfied that the book is obscene, you must go on to the further question: are the merits of the book as a novel *so high* that they outbalance the obscenity so its publication is *for the public good*? . . . I would repeat the observation made by Mr Griffith-Jones who said, "Keep your feet on the ground." In other words, do not allow yourselves to get lost in the higher realms of literature, education, sociology and ethics.

'One witness, Mrs Bennett, said, "A reader who is capable of understanding Lawrence could get much of what his view is." Who, members of the jury, are the people capable of understanding Lawrence? You have to think of people with no literary background, with little or no learning . . .

'It has been said that the book does not deal simply and solely with sexual relationships, but that it deals with other matters, such as the industrial state of the country and the hard lives people are living. Whether you find there is very much in the book about that or not is for you to say . . . You may ask yourselves whether, unless a person is an authority on literature, he would be able to read into the book the many different things the many witnesses said he intended to be in the book . . .

'Mrs Bennett said that Lawrence believed that marriage, not in the legal sense, but the union of two people for a lifetime was of the highest importance. Members of the jury, what is marriage if it is not in the legal sense? What are they talking about? This is a Christian country, and right through Christianity there has been lawful marriage, even if it is only before a registrar.

'The Bishop of Woolwich said Lawrence was

trying to portray the sex relationship as something sacramental.' The Judge looked up, '*Where are we getting*? Do *you* find that the author was trying to portray sex as something sacramental? Then we had the Master of the Temple, and he was full of praise for the book. Then we had Professor Pinto who said that in some measure it was a moral tract – does *that* coincide with *your* view? Do you find that the relationship between Lady Chatterley and the gamekeeper was really moral? Did you find one spark of affection between these two? Or were they merely having sexual intercourse and enjoying it?

'You heard one witness say that it is possible to feel "reverence for a man's balls"; what do you make of that? Does it coincide with your view of the matter? Well, members of the jury, there it is, there it is . . . You must ask yourselves whether as you *read* the book, you find you can agree with all the things the witnesses said Lawrence was trying to say . . . You are not bound by the evidence – you have to make up your own minds.'

Well, and so they did.

The world now knows that verdict, but for us, who waited on that day, it was a long three hours before we heard – still incredulous in relief – those words: Not Guilty. A ripple of applause broke out, stentoriously suppressed; there was no other comment. It is customary for the Judge to express thanks to the jury; Mr Justice Byrne did not do so, and the words were spoken by the Clerk.

DAUNT BOOKS

Founded in 2010, the Daunt Books imprint is
dedicated to discovering brilliant works by
talented authors from around the world.
Whether reissuing beautiful new editions of lost
classics or introducing fresh literary voices, we're
drawn to writing that evokes a strong sense of
place – novels, short fiction, memoirs, travel
accounts, and translations with a lingering
atmosphere, a thrilling story, and a distinctive
style. With our roots as a travel bookshop,
the titles we publish are inspired by the
Daunt shops themselves, and the exciting
atmosphere of discovery to be found
in a good bookshop.

For more information, please visit
www.dauntbookspublishing.co.uk